Treasure Island

by Robert Louis Stevenson

Abridged and adapted by Jenny Gray

Illustrated by David Grove

A PACEMAKER CLASSIC

FEARON/JANUS/QUERCUS
Belmont, California

Simon & Schuster Education Group

Other Pacemaker Classics

ISBN 0-8224-9230-X
Library of Congress Catalog Card Number: 70-133537

Printed in the United States of America.

10 9 8 7 6 5

Contents

I The Admiral Benbow Inn

Squire Trelawney and Doctor Livesey asked me to write this book. They said I should write about the *Hispaniola*. They asked me to tell about Long John Silver. And they told me to write down everything I know about Treasure Island.

And that I will do. I will tell all that happened. There is only one thing I will *not* tell. And that is *where* Treasure Island is. That I will never tell anyone. For there is still treasure there for the taking. And enough lives have already been lost over it.

Jim Hawkins is my name. And my story begins in the year 1763. At that time, my father ran the Admiral Benbow Inn. The Admiral Benbow was at Black Hill Cove. That is on the English coast near Beechford.

I was only a boy then. But I saw many things take place there. I will tell you about some of them. They were very strange happenings. And they all took place in a very short time.

It all started when the old sailor came to stay under our roof. I can close my eyes and see him now! He was a tall, nut-brown man, strong and heavy. His long, dark hair was tied back behind his head. And an old sword cut lined one side of his face.

He was singing this song as he walked along the road.

"Fifteen men on the Dead Man's Chest—
Yo-ho-ho, and a bottle of rum!"

He stopped in front of the Admiral Benbow. He looked around for a minute. Then he walked in. "Do many people come up this way?" he asked my father. His voice was rough. It told of many hard years at sea.

"No," answered my father. "I wish they did. But the Admiral Benbow is too far away from town."

"Then this is the place for me," said the sailor. "I don't need much to keep me going. Rum I'll want, and my food. And a place to watch for ships." He threw down three or four gold pieces. "This will pay my way for a while. You can tell me when I have used it up."

Soon after that, a man came from town with a sea chest. He carried it up to the old sailor's room. It was a very big sea chest. And it looked very heavy. I wondered what was in it.

Then I heard my father talking to the man from town. "Where did the sailor come from?" he asked.

"Who knows?" answered the man from town. "He is new to the town. He asked me about a place to stay. Said he was looking for a room away from town. But he wanted to be close to the sea. That is why I told him about the Admiral Benbow."

And that is how the Captain, as we called him, came to stay with us. He was quiet and kept to himself most of the time. All day he was out watching the sea for ships. After dinner, he would sit by the fire and drink rum. When people came to the Admiral Benbow, he would hide. And he would wait to see who they were before he came out.

"Listen, boy," he said to me one day. "Would you like to make some money?"

"Yes," I said. "But how?"

"Keep an eye out for a sailor with one leg," he said. "Let me know if you see anyone like that."

"With one leg?" I asked. I wanted to be sure I had heard him right.

"Yes," he said. "I'll pay you. But keep quiet about it. No one is to know but you and me."

I thought a lot about the man with one leg. It was funny how just thinking about him made my mouth go dry. Though I had never seen him, I was afraid of him.

The Captain stayed with us for a long time. Sometimes he had bad nights. He would drink too much rum. Then he would tell ugly stories about pirates and killing.

Sometimes he banged on the table and roared out his old sea song.

> "Fifteen men on the Dead Man's Chest—
> Yo-ho-ho, and a bottle of rum!"

The Captain made trouble in another way, too. He would not pay his bill. My father asked him for money many times. But he would only look angry and say nothing.

It was around this time that my father took sick. My mother put him to bed and sent for Doctor Livesey.

That night was one of the old sailor's bad nights. He was drinking and singing, and banging on the table. Doctor Livesey could not help hearing all this noise. He came down to tell the Captain to be quiet. He told him that there was a sick man in the house. But the Captain would not be quiet. He started telling his ugly stories of pirates on the high seas.

Doctor Livesey did not want to hear such stories. And he told the Captain so. "I have one thing to say to you," he went on. "If you keep on drinking rum, you will soon be dead. Then we will all be better off."

This made the Captain angry. He jumped to his feet and pulled out a knife. I thought he was going to kill Doctor Livesey then and there.

But Doctor Livesey was not afraid of him. He kept right on talking to the Captain in the same cold voice.

"Put away that knife this minute," he said. "Put it away or I'll have a rope around your neck."

The two men looked each other straight in the eye. Then the sailor put away his knife. He sat down, talking to himself.

"You seem to be the kind who would do anything," Doctor Livesey went on. "You would cut a man down over nothing. If I hear that you are making trouble, you will know it. I'll have you hunted down like a dog. Watch your step!"

With that, Doctor Livesey got his horse and rode away. The Captain made no more trouble that night. And he was quiet for many days after.

It was a bad winter for us at the Admiral Benbow. It was very cold. And few people came to the inn. My father showed no sign of getting well. So my mother and I had to run the place alone. We had little time to think about the old sailor.

2 The Visit of Black Dog

One morning when I was working in the inn, the front door banged open. In walked a strange, gray-faced man. He was tall and thin. I had never seen him before.

"What can I do for you, sir?" I asked.

"Well, my boy," he said. "I want to find my old shipmate, Bill. Billy Bones, we called him." He showed his long yellow teeth in a smile. "Could he be staying here?"

"There is a sailor staying here," I said. "But I don't know what his name is. We call him the Captain."

"You might well call Billy by that name," said the man. "Now Billy Bones is a right ugly man," he went on. "He has an old sword cut down one side of his face. Does that sound like your Captain?"

"Yes, it does," I answered.

"It does, now!" he cried. "And where might the Captain be at this minute?"

"He is walking on the beach," I answered. "He will be back soon."

"Oh, he will?" said the man. "Then I think I'll wait for him. I'll give him a little surprise. I'll hide behind the door."

7

Before long, the old sailor came marching in. He banged the door shut behind him.

"Bill?" cried the tall, thin man. "Billy Bones?"

The Captain turned at once. His eyes grew very big. Then he took on the look of a tired, sick old man.

"Come, Bill, you know me," said the man. "You know your old shipmate. One of Captain Flint's old crew, I was."

"Black Dog!" cried the Captain, his voice shaking.

"Who else?" said the man. "Black Dog it is. And I have come to see my old shipmate, Billy Bones. I thought we could talk about old times."

"All right," said the Captain, "you found me. You have caught up with me at last. Well, then, let me have the bad news. What do you want?"

"I want to talk, Bill. Nothing more," said Black Dog, smiling. "We will just sit and talk, like old ship-mates."

Then the Captain told me to go, and to leave the door wide open.

They talked for a long time. I tried to hear what they were saying. But I could not make it out.

"No, no, no!" the Captain cried at last. "If it comes to swinging, all of us swing, I say."

All at once, there were many loud noises. Chairs and tables were being knocked around. Then came the sound of swords hitting one another. Black Dog went racing out the front door. The Captain was right behind him, cutting at the air with his sword.

But Black Dog was too fast for the Captain. He ran off down the road and got away. The old sailor stood at the door watching him. Then he turned back to me. He held his hand over his eyes a minute.

"Bring me a bottle of rum, Jim," he said. Then he felt his way back into the room.

"Did he hurt you?" I asked.

"Rum!" he roared. "I must get away from here. Rum! Rum!"

I ran to get the rum. But when I came back, the Captain was down on the floor.

I did not know what to do. Was he hurt? Was he dead?

Just then, Doctor Livesey came to visit my father. He looked first at me. Then he looked down at the Captain. "What is going on here?" he asked.

"Oh, Doctor Livesey," I cried. "You are just in time. The Captain has been hurt!"

"Hurt?" said the doctor. "He has hurt himself with all that rum. I told him this would happen."

Doctor Livesey did what he could to help the Captain. After a while, the old sailor opened his eyes.

"Now listen to me," Doctor Livesey said to him. "Rum is no good for you. Leave it alone. If you drink any more, it will kill you."

Doctor Livesey and I helped the Captain to his room. Then the doctor took me to one side. "Make him stay in bed for about a week," he told me. "That is the best thing for him. And no more rum! Another attack will kill him."

After lunch, I stopped by the Captain's door. He had been sleeping for a long time. But now he was sitting up in bed. Still, he did not look at all strong.

"Jim," he said, "bring me a drink of rum, will you? Just a little one?"

"The doctor . . . , " I began.

But he started to curse the doctor. "That yellow dog of a doctor! What does he know?"

He was making a lot of noise. He started banging on the table next to his bed. I thought about my father. He was very sick and needed quiet.

"I'll get you one small drink," I said. And when I brought it, he pulled it right out of my hand. It was gone in one quick drink.

"Jim," he said after a few minutes, "come close to me. . . . You know that man who came today?"

"The one who called you Billy Bones?" I asked.

"Yes," said the sailor. "That was Black Dog."

"Is your name Billy Bones?" I asked.

"Yes," said the Captain. "Flint's crew knew me as Billy Bones." He took a quick look around the room. "That Black Dog is a bad one, Jim," he said. "And the others are just as bad."

"What others?" I asked. "Why are they after you? What will they do?"

The Captain only rolled his eyes.

"Will they kill you?" I asked.

"They may," he said. "And then again they may not. They will give me the Black Spot, though. That they will do. That is what I am afraid of most."

I did not know what he was talking about. "What is the Black Spot?" I asked.

"The Black Spot is a sign, Jim. It is a sign of trouble to come. Let it go at that. Jim, if they come again, they will go for my sea chest."

His sea chest, I thought. What is in his sea chest? Does he have money there?

But the Captain was still talking. "If those men come," he went on, "go get that doctor. Tell him to bring help. Black Dog and the others, they sailed with old Flint, they did. I was Flint's right-hand man. I helped him hide the treasure. It is all there on the island. And I am the only one who knows where it is. Now the rest of them want to know. But they never will—not if I can help it."

The Captain pushed himself up from the bed with one arm. "Now be sure you do what I say, Jim," he said. "Keep your eyes open, and I will save part of the treasure for you. On my word!"

The Captain fell back on his bed. Soon he went into a deep sleep.

That same night, my father died. Nothing else seemed to matter then. I was busy taking care of my mother. And I was running the Admiral Benbow Inn. I had no time to think about the Captain.

3 The Black Spot

Late one cold, wet afternoon, I was standing in front of the inn. I was feeling very bad. I was thinking of my poor dead father. Just then, I heard a strange tapping noise. I looked up and saw a blind man coming along the road. He was tapping his way with a long stick.

The blind man stopped in front of me. I had never seen such an ugly old man before. His back had a great bump in it. And his clothes were old and full of holes.

"Will any kind friend help me?" he called. "Will anyone tell me where I am? Help a man who lost his eyes for his country. For England! In what part of that country am I now?"

"You are at the Admiral Benbow Inn, sir," I said. "You are at Black Hill Cove."

"I hear a voice," he said. "It is a boy's voice. Please give me your hand, boy. Will you take me in? Will you?"

I was afraid of this ugly old man. But he was blind and needed my help. So, I held out my hand to him. The old man caught my arm and held it. I tried to get away. But I could not break his hold.

"Now, boy," he said in a rough voice. "Take me to Bill. Take me in to Billy Bones."

"Billy Bones, sir?" I asked, my voice shaking. "There is no Billy Bones here, sir. There is no man by that name here."

The blind man's nails were digging into my skin. "Do as I say, boy," he said. "This is the Admiral Benbow Inn. I know Bill is here."

Though he was hurting my arm, I tried not to cry out. "But, sir," I said, "he is a sick man."

"Come on!" said the blind man, in an angry voice. "Move! Take me to Billy Bones."

There was nothing I could do. I had to take him up to the Captain's room.

The Captain was sitting in his chair. He was alone, as always. When he saw us come in, his face went white. He tried to pull himself up. "Pew!" he cried. "Old blind Pew! Not you again. After all these years!"

"Yes," said the blind man, walking over to the Captain. "It is me. At last I have found you, Billy Bones. And now I must give you this."

The blind man felt for the Captain's hand. When he found it, he put something in it. Then, before I knew what was happening, he turned and left the room.

The Captain opened his hand. He seemed almost afraid to look. But he did look. In his hand was a small round piece of paper.

"Oh, no!" cried the Captain, getting up from his chair. "Not that!" Then he fell down on the floor.

I ran to him at once. He was not moving. I did not know what to do. I called to my mother, and she ran to help me. But it was no use. The Captain was dead.

I felt very bad. I had liked the old sailor. It was all too much for me. First my father had died and now the Captain. All at once, I began to cry.

Near the Captain's hand lay the round piece of paper the blind man gave him. I picked it up. And right away I saw what it was. One side of the paper was painted black.

"The Black Spot!" I cried. "Mother, they gave him the Black Spot! He said they would."

"Look!" said my mother, turning the paper over. "There is writing on the back."

Together, we read what it said: "We will come for you after dark."

"What is this all about?" my mother asked. "Who is coming for the Captain?"

"Black Dog and Pew, the blind man!" I cried. "And there may be others with them. The Captain said they would come after him."

"But why?" asked my mother. "Who are they? And how do they know the Captain?"

"The Captain was their shipmate," I answered. "They were all pirates, the lot of them. The Captain knew about a buried treasure. But he would not tell them where it was."

I looked at my mother. She looked at me. I could tell what she was thinking. We had been counting on getting money from the Captain for his bill. But now that he was dead . . .

Then I thought of what the Captain told me the day Black Dog came. "His sea chest!" I cried. "He said they would go after his sea chest. He might have some money there."

I did not want to take money from a dead man. But we needed it. And it belonged to us by right.

I pointed to the sea chest in a corner of the Captain's room. "Let's go through his sea chest," I said. "But we must hurry. It is getting dark. Those men may be here any minute."

At first, I had trouble opening the sea chest. I thought I would have to break it open. But then something gave way, and I got it open.

The sea chest was filled with many things. On top, there was a suit of clothes that looked almost new. Under the suit, we found two guns and more clothes. With the clothes, there was a fine old Spanish watch. We also found five or six beautiful shells of some strange sea animals.

But we found what we were after at the bottom of the chest. It was a bag full of gold pieces! And next to the bag of gold pieces were some papers. They were tied together with string.

My mother took the bag of gold pieces from the sea chest. "I'll take only what belongs to us," she said. And she began to count out the money.

She was still counting when I heard a sound that turned my blood cold. Tapping! I heard the tapping of the blind man's stick on the road. He was coming back!

I put my hand on my mother's arm. She listened and heard the tapping too.

"What is it?" she asked. "What is the matter?"

"Don't talk," I said. "It is Pew, the blind man who gave the Captain the Black Spot. He is coming back to get the sea chest."

4 The Pirates

The tapping sound stopped at the door to the inn. Then there was tapping on the door. Next we heard the blind man trying to open the door.

We sat very still and said nothing. After a while, the tapping blind man left the inn. He headed up the road.

Both of us jumped to our feet. "We must get away from here!" cried my mother. "He will come back with the others."

My mother threw the bag with the rest of the gold into the sea chest. Then she ran from the room. Without thinking, I hurried after her. I carried the Captain's papers with me.

We hurried down to the front door of the inn. Once outside, we ran down the road as fast as we could.

And we were not a minute too soon. We had not gone far down the road when we heard men running.

"Quick!" I cried. "Run into the woods, Mother. Hide behind the trees."

We ran off the road and dropped to the ground behind a big tree. From where we hid, we could see and hear everything.

Six or seven men came racing to the door of the inn. I thought I could see the blind man following behind them. I was right, for the next thing I heard was his voice. "Down with the door!" he cried. "Break it down!"

Then other voices rang out with rough curses. Heavy blows fell on the front door of the Admiral Benbow Inn. Soon the door gave way.

"Go up to his room!" cried the blind man. "Get his sea chest!"

We heard the sound of feet racing up to the Captain's room. Then one of the men threw open a window. "Bill is dead!" he called down.

Then another man called from the window. "Someone got here before us, Pew," he said. "They took everything out of his sea chest. But there is some money here."

"Curse the money," roared the blind man. "What about the map? Is it there?"

"No," called one of the men. "We can not find it."

"It was that boy and his mother!" cried the blind man. "Curse them both! I should have put their eyes out."

"Find them," he went on. "They must be hiding in there. Pull the place to pieces if you have to."

From our hiding place in the woods, we heard the men hunting for us. They were going through every room of the inn. We could hear them pushing over tables and chairs.

We were very much afraid. We knew that soon they would come looking for us in the woods.

But just then we heard horses coming along the road. The men in the inn heard the horses, too.

"The law is after us!" cried one of them.

"They must have followed us!" cried another man.

"Quick! Back to the ship!" called the first man out the door.

The men were running up the road now—all but the blind man. He could not keep up with them. He was tapping and hopping along behind them. "Black Dog! Johnny!" he cried. "Come back! Don't leave old Pew behind. Not your old shipmate!"

But the men did not come back. And they did not wait for old Pew. Soon the blind man's cries were lost in the noise made by the horses. Then, out of the dark night, rode ten men on horses. They were the officers of the law! They rode right by the spot where my mother and I were hiding. They rode right by the inn. And they rode down old Pew on the road!

When they saw what they had done, they came to a stop. I ran from the woods and up the road to them.

"This one is dead," said Mr. Dance, one of the officers. "Which way did the others go?" he asked me.

"Back to their ship!" I cried. "They said they had a ship."

"Follow them, men," said Mr. Dance. "They must be down by the Point."

With that, the officers of the law rode off after the pirates.

5 The Map

I ran back down the road to where my mother was still hiding. "The pirates are gone, Mother," I called. "You can come out now."

My mother came out to the road. But she was still very much afraid. She did not want to go back to the Admiral Benbow. Then we heard someone riding down the road. It was Mr. Dance.

Mr. Dance stopped and got off his horse when he saw us. "The woods were too dark," he said. "My men could not catch up with the pirates. They got away—all but that one." He pointed to Pew, who was still on the road.

I told Mr. Dance my story as we walked back to the inn. I told him about the Captain and his sea chest. I told him about Black Dog's visit. I told him about Pew and the Black Spot.

Mother and I were sick at what we found inside the inn. Doors had been knocked down. Every table and chair was turned over. And the kitchen floor was covered with bits and pieces of dishes.

Nothing had been left standing in the Captain's room. Even his bed had been cut to pieces. We found things from his sea chest here and there. But the rest of the gold was gone.

"They got the money, you say?" asked Mr. Dance. "Well, then, Hawkins, what else were they looking for? More money?"

"No, sir, not money," I answered. "I believe I have what they were looking for."

I held up the papers I took from the Captain's sea chest. "I would like to take these papers to Doctor Livesey," I said. "He can tell me what I should do with them."

"To be sure," said Mr. Dance. "The doctor is a good man. I am going back to town right now. I want to tell Squire Trelawney all that has happened. If you like, Hawkins, I'll take you along. Then we will go to see the good doctor."

I thanked him and told my mother I would be home again soon. Then Mr. Dance helped me up on his horse and we rode off.

We rode hard all the way. Soon we came to Squire Trelawney's big house. We jumped down, and Mr. Dance knocked on the door. "I am Mr. Dance," he said to the man who opened the door. "I must see the squire at once."

"The squire is with Doctor Livesey in the sitting room," said the man. And then he took us down a long hall. At the end of the hall was a large room. There, in front of a bright fire, stood the squire and the doctor.

I had never been this close to a squire before. He was a big man, over six feet tall. And he had a rough-and-ready look. His quick eyes seemed to take everything in.

"Mr. Dance, come in!" said the squire.

"Hello, Dance," said the doctor. "And hello to you, Jim. What brings you here so late?"

Mr. Dance stood up very straight and told his story. He told about one of his men spotting the pirates' ship. Then he told how he and his men went after the pirates at the inn. He also told what he had learned about the pirates from me.

At last Mr. Dance finished talking.

"You have done a good day's work, sir," said the squire. "And as for that blind man, Pew, don't feel bad. We are all better off with him dead. Now you must have a drink before you leave."

"And so, Jim," said Doctor Livesey, turning to me. "You think you have some papers the pirates were after?"

"Here they are, sir," I said. And I handed him the papers I took from the Captain's sea chest.

The doctor took the papers. He looked as if he wanted to look at them right away. But he put them in his coat pocket.

After a while, Mr. Dance finished his drink and left.

"Well, squire," said Doctor Livesey. "Now we should hear more from Jim. What do you think?"

"Quite right, sir," said Squire Trelawney. And both men turned to look at me.

I told them my story from the beginning. I told them everything I knew about the captain. I told them how he used to keep watch for ships. And I told about the visits of Black Dog and Pew. I said that they had all been shipmates in Captain Flint's crew. I told about the Black Spot. I finished my story by telling them about the Captain's papers. "Old Pew was very mad when he could not find them," I said. "That is why he made the other pirates hunt for me and my mother."

The squire was very pleased. "Good work, Jim!" he cried. "You tricked those pirates. And you got away to tell about it. Well done!"

The doctor turned to Squire Trelawney. "Have you heard of this man Flint before?" he asked.

"Heard of him!" roared the squire. "Why Flint was as bad a pirate as ever sailed the seas. The stories they tell of him! They would make your hair stand on end!"

"I have heard those stories," said the doctor. "But I want to know about the treasure. Have you ever heard that Captain Flint left a buried treasure?"

"You heard Jim's story," said the squire. "You know what happened at the Admiral Benbow. What else were those dogs after but treasure?"

"What about these papers?" asked the doctor. He took the papers from his coat pocket. "If there is a treasure map here, what then?"

"I'll tell you," said the squire. "If we have a map, we will hunt for the treasure. I will get us a ship and men for a full crew. If there is a buried treasure, I want to find it!"

"Very well," said Doctor Livesey. "If it is all right with Jim, we will open the Captain's papers."

I said it was fine with me. So the doctor cut the string that tied the Captain's papers. What he found was a small book inside a heavy piece of paper. Both the book and the paper seemed to be very old.

We looked at the book first. There were strange short notes in it. But these notes said nothing about a treasure.

We opened out the piece of heavy paper. And yes, it *was* what we were looking for! It was a map of an island.

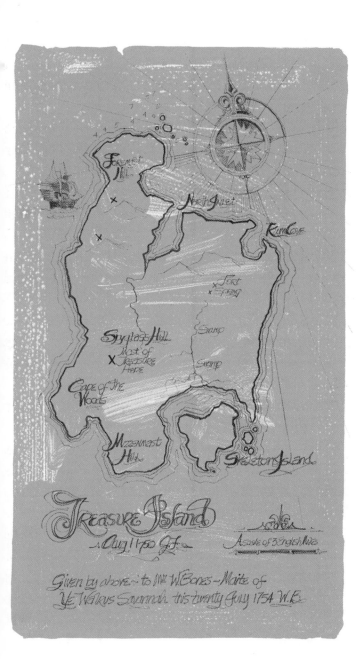

Treasure Island

Aug 1750 J.F.

A scale of 3 English Miles

Given by above ~ to Mr W. Bones Maite of
Y^e Walrus Savannah this twenty July 1754 W.B.

Doctor Livesey rubbed his hands together. The squire and I laughed.

"We have it!" cried the squire. "Now all we must do is to go to the island to get the treasure. Tomorrow I go to Bristol. In three weeks—two weeks—in ten days, I'll get us a ship. It will be the best ship and crew in England. Livesey, you will be ship's doctor. And Hawkins shall come as cabin boy!"

"You will make a fine cabin boy, Jim!" cried Doctor Livesey.

The squire was dancing around the room. "If we have good winds," he said, "we will find the island in no time. And then we will be rolling in money!"

"Yes, Trelawney," said the doctor, the smile gone from his face now. "This is all very nice—this ship of yours and the buried treasure. But there is someone around here that I am very much afraid of."

"And who is that, sir?" cried the squire. "Name the dog!"

"*You*, squire," answered the doctor. "For you can not keep quiet! We must be very careful about this map. We are not the only ones who know about it. Think of what those pirates did at the Admiral Benbow! They will stop at nothing if they find out we have the map."

"Livesey, my good man," said the squire. "You are right, as always. I will be very careful to say nothing to anyone. I will be quiet as a stone. Just you wait and see."

6 The Hispaniola

Squire Trelawney went to Bristol to get a ship and a crew. But it took him far more than ten days to do it. I waited and waited and waited. Each day I thought I would hear from him. But there was no word.

Doctor Livesey had gone to London. He was trying to find another doctor to take his place in town. This was taking time, too. Doctor Livesey was a good man. He wanted to be very careful about getting another doctor. He did not want to leave the care of his people to just anyone.

While I waited for news from Bristol, I helped my mother at the inn. There was much work to be done. The pirates had left the Admiral Benbow in a very bad way.

But I had time to think while I waited, too. I thought about the island with the buried treasure. What strange things would we find on the island? Would there be wild animals? Were there Indians on the island? I was not afraid of wild animals and Indians. But little did I know how bad things would get on the island.

At last a letter came from Squire Trelawney in Bristol.

Dear Hawkins,

I now have a ship that is ready to go to sea. She is a beautiful ship, too. The *Hispaniola* is her name.

At first, I could not find men to help me fit her out for sea. But once word got around that we were after treasure, I had no trouble.

"Oh, no!" I said out loud. "Doctor Livesey was right. The squire can not keep his mouth shut. Every man in Bristol must know we are hunting for buried treasure." But I went on with the rest of the letter.

A friend sent me a man to captain the ship. His name is Smollett. I can not say that I like him very much. But he is said to be a very good sailor.

Soon after I got the *Hispaniola*, I began to round up a crew. Never having done this before, I was having a hard time of it. But then I met a man, a very fine man. He has found me a crew in no time. Long John Silver is the man's name. I don't know what I would have done without him. And to think he just happened along at the right time!

Long John Silver has sailed all the seven seas. And he has been in many a fight. He lost one of his legs in the last war. He knows a lot about sailors. Right away, he told me that two of the crew I found were no good. So I fired them on the spot.

The crew that Silver put together is not much to look at. But they are a strong and ready lot. And Silver says that he knows each man well. He is sure we can count on them. Silver himself is coming along on the trip as ship's cook.

So, Hawkins, that is the good news. You must come to Bristol right away. I have sent a letter to Doctor Livesey in London. He is to come straight to Bristol too.

John Trelawney, Esq.

This was what I had been waiting for. At last I was to go to Bristol! You can guess how happy I was.

It was hard saying good-by to my mother. She cried. And I could not help crying a little too. We both knew that I would be gone for a long time. But I told her I would be all right. After all, I would be with the doctor and the squire. And we would have a fine ship and a good crew.

That night I got on the Bristol Mail Coach. The ride took all night. And I was asleep most of the way. It was morning when I woke up. And I was in Bristol!

Squire Trelawney was staying at an inn near the docks. I had to walk along the docks to get there.

On my way, I saw ships of all kinds. They had come from every corner of the world. And they were busy with sailors who sang as they worked.

How happy I felt! The sea air had never smelled so fresh before. I, Jim Hawkins, was going to sea! I was going off to a strange island. I was on a hunt for a buried treasure!

Squire Trelawney met me at the door of his inn. "So there you are, Hawkins," he said. "Doctor Livesey came in from London last night. Now that you are here, we can . . ."

Just then, Doctor Livesey came out of the inn. "Good to see you again, Jim," he said, shaking my hand. Then he turned to the squire. "Are we ready to board the ship now?" he asked.

"To be sure!" answered the squire. "We sail tomorrow." And without another word, he started off down the docks.

We boarded a small boat at the end of the docks. As we were rowed away from the docks, Squire Trelawney pointed out the *Hispaniola*. She *was* a pretty ship. And she rode high in the water.

Before long, we were climbing on board the *Hispaniola*. Captain Smollett was waiting for us. And right away, I saw that he and the squire did not get along well.

"I'll make it short and sweet," said Captain Smollett. "I don't like the looks of things on this ship. I don't like the crew you have brought me."

"And the ship, sir?" asked the squire, in a cold voice. "I guess you don't like her!"

Doctor Livesey did not want trouble with the captain. He tried to quiet things down. "Captain Smollett," he asked, "what is the matter? Tell us, please, sir."

"The crew tells me we sail for treasure," said Captain Smollett. "Note that, sir. The *crew* tells *me*!" He pointed a finger at Squire Trelawney. "And you, sir, told me nothing of this. Do you think that was the right thing to do?"

The squire's face grew very red. But he said nothing.

"You are quite right," said the doctor. "I can see how that would make you angry."

"Another thing," said the captain. "You seem to think hunting for treasure is some kind of game. Well, I will tell you straight. It is your lives you are playing with. And if you don't win your game, you may never see England again."

"We know what we are facing, Captain Smollett," said Doctor Livesey. "But we are not afraid. We are not children. But why do you say that you don't like the crew? Are they not good sailors?"

"I think I should have picked my own men," answered the captain. "I don't like the looks of Silver and his men."

"You have a point there," said Doctor Livesey. "Squire Trelawney should have let you help him pick a crew."

"One more thing," said the captain. "There has been far too much talk about this treasure."

"So it seems," said the doctor, giving the squire a hard look.

"I'll tell you what I heard," the captain went on. "I heard the crew say you had a map of an island. They say there are X's on the map to show where the treasure is buried. I also heard that the island lies—" And Captain Smollett named the very place.

"I never told that to anyone!" cried the squire.

The captain did not even look at the squire. "I don't care who has the treasure map," he said. "But let the man who has it keep it to himself. No one in the crew—not even me—must know who has that map. I will not captain this ship if it gets out."

"I see your point, Captain Smollett," said Doctor Livesey. "You think there might be trouble with the crew."

"Sir," said the captain, "you put words in my mouth. I did not say we would have trouble with the crew. If I thought that, I would not take this ship to sea. It is only that I do not see things going quite right. And I ask you all to be very careful. That is all."

For a minute, no one said anything. But the doctor was looking at the squire.

"We will do as you ask," said Squire Trelawney. "But I don't think there is anything to be afraid of."

"That is up to you, sir," said Captain Smollett. And with that, he turned and went below.

"Trelawney," said the doctor, "you have found us a good man in Captain Smollett."

"I don't like the man," said Squire Trelawney. "If I were doing it all over again, I would pick someone else."

"Well," said the doctor, "we shall see."

7 Long John Silver

Late in the afternoon, the crew boarded the ship. I watched as their boat came to the *Hispaniola*. The men began to climb on board, quick as monkeys. They were not much to look at, as the squire said in his letter. But they seemed to know their way around a ship.

The last man to climb on board had only one leg. I knew at once that this was Long John Silver. It was his left leg that was missing. And under his left arm he used a crutch. With its help, he hopped about as light as a bird.

I watched Silver as he moved around the deck, laughing and joking with the men. He was a fine-looking man, tall and strong. Even with only one leg, he looked fit as any man.

When I first read about Silver in Squire Trelawney's letter, I was afraid of him. I thought he might be the one-legged sailor Captain Billy Bones told me about. But one look at him was enough for me. I was *sure* Silver was not the same man. After all, I had seen Black Dog and blind Pew. I knew what a pirate looked like by now! And Long John Silver did not look like one of them at all.

As I stood there, Long John Silver hopped over to me. He looked me right in the eye and smiled.

"And who might you be?" he asked.

"Jim Hawkins, sir," I answered.

"Oh, you must be our cabin boy. I am pleased to meet you," he said, shaking my hand. "I am Long John Silver."

Before I could answer, Captain Smollett and Doctor Livesey walked up.

"All right, Silver," the captain barked. "Get to work. The crew will be wanting dinner."

"Yes, sir. Right away, sir." Silver's voice was sweet as honey when he talked to the captain. With a big smile on his face, he turned and hopped away.

"Silver is a good man, captain," said Doctor Livesey.

"So it seems, doctor," answered Captain Smollett. Then he turned to me. "You, Hawkins," he said, "go below to the kitchen. Get to work!" So, I hurried off after Long John Silver.

It was a good thing I was used to hard work. There was a lot of work to be done on the *Hispaniola*. All night long before we left, we stored the ship's goods in place. I was dog-tired.

Tired as I was, though, I did not want to go to bed. Everything was so strange and new on board the ship. I did not want to miss anything.

At last, morning came. And the ship was ready to sail. Each man in the crew was in his place.

"Let's have a song to set sail by!" one of them cried.

"The old one!" called another.

"Right, boys," cried Long John Silver. And he began to sing a song I knew too well.

"Fifteen men on the Dead Man's Chest," he sang.

Then the rest of the crew sang, "Yo-ho-ho and a bottle of rum!"

Hearing this song made me think again of Captain Billy Bones. I could see him sitting in the Admiral Benbow. I heard him roaring out that same song.

But I did not think of Captain Billy Bones for long. The wind filled the *Hispaniola*'s sails. Then the docks and the other ships grew small. The *Hispaniola* was headed out to sea. We were on our way to Treasure Island!

8 The Apple Barrel

All in all, it was a good trip. The ship was a good ship, and the men were good sailors.

I worked beside Long John Silver every day. Soon we became good friends. Every man in the crew liked him. He was a good cook. And he kept his kitchen bright and clean.

In a corner of the kitchen, he kept a parrot in a cage. "Sit down, Hawkins," Long John would say. "Sit down and have a talk with me. Now here is Captain Flint. I call my parrot Captain Flint after the great pirate. This bird is a good old sailor. How old he is, no one knows. Parrots live a long, long time."

And the parrot would cry, "Pieces of eight! Pieces of eight! Pieces of eight!"

Captain Smollett and Squire Trelawney did not get along any better as time went on. But the captain liked the crew and the ship better than he did at first. He said they did their work and gave him no trouble. And he was more than happy with the *Hispaniola*. "She takes to sailing like a duck takes to water," he would say. "But," he would go on, "we still have a long way to go. And I don't like this trip!"

Squire Trelawney was good to the crew. Too good, Captain Smollett said. The squire saw that there was always a big barrel of apples in the kitchen. When a sailor was hungry, he took as many apples as he wanted.

"Never knew good to come of anything like that," Captain Smollett told Doctor Livesey.

But good did come of the apple barrel, as you shall see. Without it, we would never have learned what the crew was up to. We might have been killed in our beds! This is how it came about.

It was the last day of our trip. The sea was quiet. And the men on deck were watching for signs of the island.

I was all alone in the kitchen. Dinner was over, and the kitchen had been cleaned. I had finished my work for the day. I wanted to have an apple before I went to bed. But there seemed to be no apples left in the big barrel. To make sure, I climbed inside it to feel around the bottom.

Before I could climb out again, I heard some men coming into the kitchen. One of the men began to talk. It was Long John Silver. Before he said ten words, I knew I had to stay put and keep quiet.

"No, not I," said Silver. "Flint was our captain. I was only a ship's officer, same as Pew and Billy Bones. I lost my leg in the same fight that took Pew's eyes."

"Captain Flint was a good man, to be sure," said another man. "And soon we will have our hands on his gold!"

"Look here, Silver," said another man. "How long do I have to put up with Smollett? That man is hard to take."

"You will just have to wait until I tell you, Dick," answered Silver. "I'll give the word when the time comes. Wait until they get us to the island and find the treasure."

"What will we do with Trelawney and the rest of them?" asked Dick.

"What do you think, Israel?" Silver asked the first man. "Should we leave them on the island? Or should we cut them down? That would have been Flint's way—or Billy Bones'!"

"Billy was the man for that," said Israel. " 'Dead men don't talk,' Billy always said."

"And I go along with Billy on that," said Silver. "That way, there will be no one to talk when we get back to England. But wait until I give you the word! And now, Dick, be a good boy. Put your arm in the barrel and get me an apple."

Hearing this made my blood run cold. If the pirates found me in the barrel, they would kill me! I knew I had to get away. The lives of all the good men on the ship were in my hands. I wanted to jump out of the barrel and run. But I was too afraid to move! I lay there, shaking and waiting.

I heard Dick get up. Then Israel stopped him. "Apples!" he cried. "Who wants apples at a time like this? We want rum, Long John!"

"All right, boys," said Silver, laughing. And he told Dick where to find the rum.

I began to think that I would never get away. But I was saved by what happened next. Up on the deck, one of the crew called out. "Land ho!" he cried. "I see the island!"

9 Treasure Island

The cry of "Land ho!" saved me. Silver and his men ran up to the deck. They all wanted to see the island.

I waited until they had gone. Then I jumped out of the barrel and followed them up to the deck.

All of the men were on the deck now. They were standing along the side of the ship, talking and pointing. The sun was setting and it was getting dark. But I, too, could see the island. It was a strange and ugly place. No one but pirates would ever visit here, I thought.

Doctor Livesey was standing outside his cabin. He was talking to Captain Smollett and the squire. I hurried over to him.

"Doctor," I said, "I have something to tell you all." I kept my voice down so the sailors could not hear me. "It is about the crew."

"Let's go into my cabin," said the doctor.

When we got inside, Doctor Livesey closed the door.

"Well, Hawkins," said Squire Trelawney, "you have something to say about the crew? What is it?"

I told them how I happened to climb into the apple barrel. And I told them everything I heard while I was hiding there. "Silver sailed with Captain

Flint, the pirate," I said. "He and Billy Bones and Pew were Flint's officers. All of the crew he brought on board are pirates, too. He is going to take the treasure away from us. Then we are all going to be killed!"

"That dog Silver!" said the squire. "I would like to see him swinging at the end of a rope!"

"We all would," said the captain. "But first we must make some plans of our own. And I think I know what we should do."

"Let's hear it!" said the squire and the doctor.

"These pirates will kill us if we make them turn back now," said the captain. "So we must go on to the island. But they do not plan to kill us until the treasure is found. That gives us time to plan a way to fight them."

"Fight them?" asked the doctor. "How?"

"I am coming to that," Captain Smollett went on. "Can we count on the men that *you* brought on board, squire?"

"To be sure!" answered the squire.

"Good," said Captain Smollett. "We must make careful plans. We will wait for the right time. Then we will attack them before they can attack us!"

"You have the matter well thought out, captain," said Squire Trelawney. "I will tell my three men at once. But even with their help, that leaves only six men on our side. The pirates have three times as many!"

"But we have Jim, too," said Doctor Livesey. "He can be more help to us than anyone. The pirates will not be as careful around him. If he keeps his eyes open, he may find out what their plans are."

"Hawkins, we are counting on you!" said the squire.

I was not too happy to hear this. After all, what could I do? But as it turned out, I *was* the one who saved us.

Next morning I got a better look at the island. I must say, I liked it no more than I had the day before. That is to say, I did not like it at all. It gave me a strange feeling.

Strange things began to happen on the ship, too. The men were slow to do their work. They cursed the captain and one another. Fights would break out here and there. I saw Long John Silver going from one man to another. He seemed to be quieting them down. Yes, I thought, he is telling them to wait. He is telling them that the time is not right.

Captain Smollett did not like the way things were going. "The crew is getting ugly," he told us. "They want to go to the island. If I don't let them, they may attack us right away. I am going to let them take two of the boats."

"Do as you think best, captain," said the squire.

That day, we anchored in a place where the water was not deep. We lay between Treasure Island and a small island called Skeleton Island. Then Captain Smollett called the crew together. "Men," he said, "we have made a long trip and you are tired. You can take the day off and go to the island."

When they heard this, the men were very happy. They laughed and joked as they let down the boats. They were ready to go in no time at all. They took one of the squire's men with them. But they were leaving three of their own men on the ship.

Then it came to my head to go with them to the island. To this day, I don't know why. But as it turned out, it helped to save our lives!

I jumped into one of the boats just as it pulled away from the ship. Only one man saw me. All he said was, "Sit down so you don't rock the boat, Jim." Not even my friends on the ship knew I had gone.

The boats raced for the island. The minute my boat landed, I jumped out. Then I ran for the jungle. But I was not quick enough. Silver had seen me. "Jim, Jim!" he cried. "Where are you going, Jim?"

I ran into the jungle as fast as I could. I jumped over rocks. And I ducked under tree branches. I heard a gun fired and a man cry out. That must be the squire's man, I thought. They have killed him!

I ran until I could run no more. Then I stopped and listened for Long John's voice. Minutes went by, and I heard no one. The only sounds were the cries of the jungle birds. I was alone in the jungle.

For the first time, I looked around me. What a strange place, I thought. The jungle was dark, for the trees kept out the sun. Here and there, bright-colored flowers grew. But they were not pretty, like the flowers at home.

Walking along, I saw many little ponds with wild ducks. And I could hear frogs calling to each other.

At last, the trees began to thin out. I was tired and hot. So I stopped to rest at the bottom of a big hill.

The side of the hill was covered with small stones. As I sat there, something moved on the hill, sending stones sliding down at me. I looked up just in time to see something duck behind a tree. What it was, I could not tell. But it was big and wild-looking, like a great monkey.

10 Ben Gunn

I was cut off on both sides. Behind me were the pirates. And in front of me was some strange wild animal!

I turned and ran beside the hill. At once, the animal followed me. Then it raced from tree to tree, always coming out in front of me. I could not get away from it, no matter which way I turned.

At last, I stopped and waited to see what would happen next. I did not have to wait long. The thing peeped out at me from behind a tree. Then it came out into the open.

I could see now that it was not an animal at all. It was a man! His face and arms were dark brown from the sun. And he was dressed in animal skins.

"Who are you?" I cried.

"Ben Gunn," he answered in a strange voice. "I am poor Ben Gunn, I am. And I have talked with no man in three years."

"Three years!" I cried. "All alone! Did your ship go down?"

"No," he said. "I was left here by my shipmates. My ship went off without me. I have lived on goats and fruit and what fish I could catch. But I had no one to talk to. That is what I missed most. What are you called, boy?"

"Jim," I told him.

"Jim? I like that name. Well now, Jim," he said, drawing close to me, "tell me something. Would that be Flint's ship sitting off the island?"

"No," I said. "It is not Flint's ship. Flint is dead. But many of Flint's men are in the crew."

"Not a man with one leg!" he cried.

"Long John Silver?" I asked.

"Yes, Silver! That was his name," he said.

"Silver is the cook," I said. "And it seems he is the real captain of the ship."

Then I began to tell Ben Gunn the story of our trip. When I had finished, he patted me on the head. "You are a good boy, Jim," he said. "But you and your friends are in real trouble.

"Flint's men will kill you all for that treasure. I know, because I once sailed with them. I was on Flint's ship when he brought the treasure here. He took six men and the treasure with him to this island. He used the men to help him bury the treasure. Then he killed them all. How he did it, no one knows! He came back to the ship alone. And then we sailed away to get more treasure."

"But how did you get on this island?" I asked.

"That was three years back," he answered. "I was on another ship that was sailing near here. I talked the captain into landing here to hunt for the treasure. We looked for two weeks. But we did not find even one piece of gold! The men were very angry. To get even with me, they sailed off and left me here alone."

"You must have had a hard time," I said. "Three years is a long time to be alone."

"Oh, I kept busy, I did," he said, with a strange laugh. "But tell me, would your friends take me back to England with them? If I was to help them, that is?"

"I *know* they would!" I said. "Doctor Livesey and Squire Trelawney are good men. But I don't even know if I will ever see them again. I can not get back to the *Hispaniola*. Silver and his men have the boats."

"So they do," said Ben Gunn. "But I can take care of that. I have a boat of my own. I made it from wood and skins. I hide it behind a big white rock down on the beach. It is not far from the place you landed. When it gets dark, we can—"

His last words were cut off by the roar of a big gun being fired.

"What was that?" he asked.

"I think it was the ship's gun!" I cried. "My friends must be in trouble." I turned to run back the way I had come.

But Ben Gunn took me by the arm. "Not that way!" he said. "I know a place where we can see what is going on. No one can see us from there. Follow me!"

I followed Ben Gunn to the top of a hill. From there, we could see the *Hispaniola*.

I did not like what I saw. Three of Silver's men were on the deck of the *Hispaniola*. They were loading the ship's gun.

Then I saw my friends. They were in a small boat loaded down with heavy boxes. The boat had stopped not far from the beach.

"They are not moving!" I cried. And then we saw why. While the others held the boat still, Squire Trelawney pointed his gun at the *Hispaniola*. He fired, and one of the pirates fell to the deck. The other pirates ducked away from the *Hispaniola's* gun.

At once, the men in the small boat began to row with all their might. Seeing this, the pirates hurried back and loaded the *Hispaniola's* gun.

"Your friends' trouble is just beginning," said Ben Gunn. "Look!"

It was Silver and the rest of his men! They were heading along the beach toward my friends.

I looked back at the small boat. By now, my friends had almost rowed to the beach. But the pirates had finished loading the *Hispaniola's* gun. They fired it!

There was a loud noise and a big splash. Water covered the boat carrying my friends.

"They are hit!" I cried. "The boat is going down!"

The pirates running along the beach thought the boat had been hit, too. They stopped and began to laugh and clap one another on the back.

"Look again, Jim," cried Ben Gunn.

I looked. But I could not believe my eyes. My friends were all right. Two of them were already on

the beach. They were helping the others out of the water.

"The pirates did not hit the boat," said Ben. "It went down because it got filled with too much water."

When Silver and his men saw my friends on the beach, they began cursing. Then they started running down the beach after them. But my friends were too fast for them. They helped the last man from the water and headed for the jungle. With angry cries, the pirates raced after them.

"They are heading for the fort," said Ben Gunn. "Over there!" He pointed to a spot in the jungle. Following his hand, I could see the top of a building of some kind. But the trees hid most of it.

The minutes went by. How many, I don't know. They seemed like years to me. Then we heard the sound of many guns being fired. But the firing stopped almost as fast as it started. Everything was quiet.

"The fight is over," I said. "But how do we know which side has the fort? We can not see anything from here."

"We will just have to wait for a sign," said Ben Gunn.

"A sign?" I asked. "What kind of sign? I don't . . . "

"That kind." Ben cut in, pointing to the fort.

And then I saw it. Flying over the fort was the flag of England!

II The Fort

No words can tell how happy I was to see the English flag. I wanted to go to my friends in the fort at once. But Ben Gunn stopped me. "Wait and see what the pirates do next," he said.

Soon we saw the pirates again. They came from the jungle to the beach where my friends had landed. Silver sent men into the water to bring in the boat and its stores. Then he had them carry the barrels and boxes to the beach. Other pirates he put to work getting wood and making a fire.

Silver also sent men to get the other two boats. One of them went out to the *Hispaniola*. The other one was rowed back to Silver.

"Are they going to sleep out on the beach?" I asked.

"It looks that way," Ben answered. He had a funny smile on his face. "But you can go to the fort now," he said. "Follow me. I know this island like the back of my hand."

I followed Ben into the jungle. He went so fast that I had a hard time keeping up with him. Before long, we came to an opening in the trees. From there, I could see the fort's high log fence.

"I don't see anyone around," said Ben. "Hurry over and climb the fence."

"Don't you want to go with me?" I asked.

"Not me," said Ben. "This is as far as I go."

"But why?" I asked.

"You and me get along very well, Jim," he said. "But I don't know how your friends will take to me. So I'll wait until you tell them about me. If they want me, you can tell them where to look. I'll be at the same place where you met me today."

Before I could say anything, Ben Gunn ran off into the jungle.

I looked around again to make sure no one was watching me. Then I ran to the fence and called out to my friends. In a minute, I was over the fence and with them once more.

They were very glad to see me. "What happened to you, Jim?" asked Doctor Livesey. "Are you all right?"

"I am fine," I said. "But I am very hungry!"

The doctor brought me some food. While I ate, he told me what happened on the *Hispaniola* after I left it.

Captain Smollett had called our men together, the doctor told me. It was then my friends found out that I was gone. They looked all over the ship for me. At last, they gave up and went on with the meeting.

Captain Smollett told them they would have to leave the *Hispaniola*. There was more than enough food and guns on the ship. But their water was almost gone. They would have to find a place where there was water.

Doctor Livesey took out the map of the island. The map showed a small fort. And it showed that there was a spring inside the fort. The men talked about this for a while. But then the captain told them there was no use talking about it. Going to the fort was the only way to save their lives.

First, they had to take care of the men Silver had left on the ship. This was not hard to do. The three pirates were sitting on the deck, laughing and talking. Squire Trelawney and his two men, Jack and Tom, took them by surprise. When the pirates saw guns pointed at them, they gave up at once.

The squire and his men put the pirates in a small cabin below deck. Then they boarded up the cabin door. Tom stayed outside the door to keep watch. The rest of the men let down a small boat. They loaded it with many guns and some food. Then they rowed it to the island.

Once on the island, they carried the stores to the fort.

The fort was nothing but a small log cabin with a fence around it. The cabin sat on a small hill. And there *was* a spring. It was at the bottom of the hill, between the cabin and the fence.

They left Jack to keep watch at the fort. And the other three went back to the *Hispaniola*. This time they loaded the boat with many boxes and barrels of food. When they were ready to go, they took Tom with them.

"We did not think the pirates could get out of the cabin," said Doctor Livesey. "But they did. We had not rowed far from the *Hispaniola* when we saw them on deck. They loaded the ship's gun and fired at us."

"I heard them fire the gun," I said. "Then I watched the rest from the top of a hill. I saw your boat go down. And I saw you run into the jungle with the pirates after you. But I could not see what happened at the fort."

"We got here just before the pirates," said Doctor Livesey. "They came running at us, firing their guns."

"We fired back at them," Captain Smollett put in. "Finding us well armed, they ran away—like the yellow dogs they are!"

"We killed two of the pirates," said Squire Trelawney. "But poor Tom got hit."

"Is Tom dead?" I asked.

"No," said Doctor Livesey. "But he is in a very bad way."

I had finished eating. Now it was my turn to tell what had happened to me. I told them how I had jumped into one of the boats going to the island. I told them how I ran away from Long John Silver when we got there. And I told them all about meeting Ben Gunn. "He brought me to the fort," I said.

"But he would not come in. He said you will have to go to him if you want him."

Doctor Livesey was deep in thought for a minute. "What do you think of Ben Gunn, Jim?" he asked at last. "Do you think we could count on him?"

"Ben Gunn said he would help us," I said. "And I believe him."

"We may need Ben Gunn's help very soon," said Doctor Livesey. "Most of our food was in the boat we lost."

"Enough of this talk!" said Captain Smollett. "We have work to do. The pirates may attack us again at any time. We must be ready for them when they come!"

Captain Smollett gave each of us something to do. I helped Squire Trelawney and Jack. We cleaned and loaded all the guns.

When night came, Captain Smollett called us all together in the cabin. "I don't think the pirates will give us any trouble for a while," he said. "Just listen to them!"

We could hear the loud voices of the pirates down on the beach. They were laughing and singing.

"They are drinking rum," said Doctor Livesey. "Too much rum, from the sound of things!"

"I think the rum will keep them busy all night," said Captain Smollett. "But we will keep watch just the same. The squire and I will take the first watch. The rest of you get some sleep."

12 The Pirates Attack

I was down at the spring getting water for breakfast when Jack called out. "Someone is coming!" he cried. "It is Silver himself!"

I ran back up the hill to have a look. Sure enough, Long John Silver was hopping up to the fence. He was smiling. And he was carrying a white flag!

"Stay inside the cabin, men!" said Captain Smollett. "This may be a trick." Then he called out to Silver. "Stop where you are or we will fire!"

Silver stopped at once. "I am not armed!" he cried.

"What is that old fox up to now?" Captain Smollett asked. Then he turned to us. "Doctor Livesey, watch the north side of the fort. Squire, watch the east side. Jack, watch the west." Then he called again to Silver. "What do you want, Silver?"

"The crew sent me to talk to you, Captain Smollett," answered Silver.

The Captain stepped outside the cabin. "Very well, come in," he called. "But don't try anything."

Silver came up to the fence. First, he threw his crutch over. Next, he climbed the fence. Once over, he picked up his crutch again.

"I'll come right to the point, Captain Smollett," said Silver, still smiling. "The crew is very angry.

And is it any wonder? Attacked we were, and by our own captain! First you send most of us off to the island. Next, you attack the three left on the *Hispaniola* and kill one of them. Then you kill two more at the fort. But even that was not enough for you. You had to kill two more on the beach last night!

Last night? I wondered what Silver was talking about. No one had left the fort last night. Who could have killed those two? And then I knew. Ben Gunn! Ben Gunn must have done it!

"That is enough, Silver," said Captain Smollett, in a cold voice. "We know all about you and your men. We know you are pirates. And we know you were planning to kill us! Tell me what you want and get out."

Silver was not smiling now. If looks could kill, Captain Smollett would have been a dead man. "All right, captain," he said, "I'll tell you what we want. *We want that treasure!* And we are going to get it. We know one of you has the treasure map. If you hand the map over, we will give you no trouble. If you don't, *we will kill every last one of you!*"

"Is that all?" asked the captain. "Now you listen to me. You will bring your men to the fort. All of you will lay down your arms. We will take you back to the *Hispaniola*. Then we will take you back to England to be tried as pirates. That is all I have to say to you. Now out you go!"

Silver's eyes almost popped out of his head. Roaring curses, he turned, climbed the fence, and hopped off into the jungle.

"Stay at your posts, men," said Captain Smollett. "Hawkins, stand by to load guns. Silver will be back. And he will bring his men with him."

We waited and waited for the pirates to come. But nothing happened.

"I wish they . . . , " the squire began. But before he could finish, the attack started.

The pirates fired at the fort from all sides. Our men fired back without stopping. Then, all at once, seven pirates raced out of the jungle.

Our men fired at the seven pirates again and again. Three of them fell. But the other four got over the fence and ran straight for the cabin.

"At them!" cried the pirates. "Cut them to pieces!"

Our men fired at the attacking pirates. But not one of the pirates was hit.

"Outside, men, outside!" cried Captain Smollett. "Fight them in the open! Use your swords!"

Our men picked up their swords and ran out of the cabin. I took a sword and raced out of the cabin too. In front of me, I saw a cursing pirate attack Doctor Livesey. I saw the doctor duck the pirate's blow. Then I saw the doctor give the pirate a great cut across his face.

"Around to the other side, men!" the captain cried over the noise.

I ran to the other side of the cabin. But as I turned the corner, I came face to face with a pirate. Cursing me, he cut the air with his sword. I jumped to one side and his blow missed me. But I tripped and went rolling down the hill. By the time I got to my feet, the fight was over.

Jack had killed the pirate who had been attacking me. Squire Trelawney had cut down another. And the pirate that Doctor Livesey hit was dead. Of the four pirates who had climbed the fence, only one was left. And he was now running for the fence as fast as he could.

"Don't let him get away!" cried the captain.

But before anyone could fire, the pirate was over the fence and gone.

13 A Visit to the Hispaniola

The pirates' attack was over almost as fast as it began. My friends and I still held the fort. And we had killed six of the pirates.

Both Captain Smollett and Squire Trelawney had been cut by the pirates' swords. The squire's cut was not too bad. But the captain had a deep, ugly cut down the side of one leg. And he had already lost a lot of blood. We had to help him back inside the cabin.

Inside the cabin, we found poor Tom dead on the floor. He had been killed when the pirates fired through the windows.

There was no sign of the pirates near the fort now. And the captain said they would not attack again that day. "I know those yellow dogs," he said. "It is rum they will be after now."

Doctor Livesey took care of the captain and the squire. Jack and I buried Tom. Then we rolled the dead pirates down the hill to the fence.

Late that afternoon, the doctor and the squire sat at Captain Smollett's side. The three men talked together for a long time. I was sitting with Jack at the other end of the cabin. I could not hear what they said. But I saw what was going on.

I saw Doctor Livesey stand up. He put what looked like the treasure map in his pocket. Then he loaded a gun and put on his sword. Without a word to anyone, he left the cabin.

Right away, I guessed what the doctor was up to. He was going out to find Ben Gunn! In the spot we were in, we could use his help.

Then I thought about Ben Gunn's boat. Ben had told me he kept his boat on the beach. He said it was near where I had landed on the island. He hid it behind a big white rock.

I wondered if Ben's boat was still in its hiding place. We might need it. If I could find it . . .

But I knew my friends would not let me leave the fort alone. I would have to get away without being seen. So, while the others were busy, I went to work.

First, I took a small gun and loaded it. I already had a small knife. So I felt ready for anything. Next, I walked down the hill to the spring. Then, when no one was looking, I ran to the fence. I climbed over in no time and ran into the jungle.

Before long, I came to the very place I was looking for. The big white rock was between the fort and the place I had landed. Across the water, I could see the *Hispaniola* at anchor. How beautiful she looked in the setting sun! But then I saw some of Silver's men on her deck. And she was flying the pirates' black flag!

Just then, I thought of something that made my blood turn cold. What if the pirates sailed away on the *Hispaniola?* What if they left us here on the island?

I ran from the jungle to the rock and dropped to the ground. Then I felt my way around through the tall grass and weeds.

At first, I saw no sign of a boat. But soon I came to a place where the ground was soft. I pushed the sand out of the way and found a covering of goat skins. It was like a little tent. And under the tent was Ben Gunn's boat.

The little boat was not much to look at. It was made of wood and goat skins, like the tent. And it was very small, just big enough for one man.

The boat was very light, too. I had no trouble getting it out of the hole in the ground. Then I put back the tent and covered it with sand again.

My plan had been to go right back to the fort with the boat. But now that I had the boat, I thought of another plan. I would make sure that the pirates did not sail away with the *Hispaniola!*

This was my plan. I would wait until it was dark. Then I would row Ben Gunn's boat out to the *Hispaniola.* If I cut her anchor rope, the tide would wash her on the beach.

After dark, I put the little boat into the water. I pushed it out as far as I could walk. Then I climbed in it.

From the boat, I could see two lights in the dark. One light was far down the beach. It was the big fire that Silver and his men kept going. The other light came from the *Hispaniola*. I rowed my boat straight for the Hispaniola's light.

After a few minutes, I came to the Hispaniola's side. Light from the cabin fell on the water around me. I had no trouble finding the anchor rope. I pulled out my knife and went right to work.

I worked as fast as I could. But the rope was very strong. And it was almost as big around as my leg! I had to cut it away bit by bit.

From the cabin above me came the voices of Silver's men. There were two of them. They were laughing and singing. And from the sound of it, they were drinking rum, too.

"Fifteen men on the Dead Man's Chest," they sang. "Yo-ho-ho, and a bottle of rum!"

Afraid though I was, I kept cutting away at the anchor rope. I had almost cut through. But just then, the window of the cabin banged open. One of the pirates threw something out the window. It landed beside me in the water.

I was sure I had been seen. My boat was sitting right in the light. I waited a few minutes, almost afraid to look. But nothing happened. The man went away from the window, leaving it open.

I started cutting the anchor rope again. I could hear the pirates better now. They were getting very

loud. They were angry. They were cursing and throwing things at each other.

At last I cut through the rope. And at once, I pushed my little boat away. But the *Hispaniola* began to swing around. I could not get away. She was carrying me with her as she turned!

Again I pushed against the *Hispaniola's* side. But it was no use. My little boat would not move. Any minute, I thought, the pirates will come out to see what is happening. They must have felt the ship swing around.

But no one looked out the cabin's window. And no one ran out on the deck.

I wondered what had happened to the two men in the cabin. I did not hear their voices any more. And they had been quite loud just a few minutes before. I was still not far from the cabin. I looked up at the open window. It was then that I spotted a rope hanging down from the deck.

Right away, I knew what I had to do. I must climb the rope and have a look inside the cabin. I had to find out what the pirates were doing.

I climbed up the rope in no time at all. Climbing ropes was something I had learned to do well on the *Hispaniola*. Once at the window, one look was all I needed. The two pirates were fighting! They were rolling around on the floor. And each man had a knife in his hand. No wonder they had not felt the *Hispaniola* moving!

I had seen enough. Now I wanted to get back to my boat and head for the Island. But as I climbed down the rope, the *Hispaniola* began swinging around again. She was swinging around the other way, out to sea. And as she moved, my little boat was left behind!

There was nothing I could do but climb on board the *Hispaniola*. The tide had changed. And the ship had moved fast. I was too far from my little boat to swim now. I climbed to the *Hispaniola*'s deck as she sailed out to sea.

14 My Adventure at Sea

The only light on the *Hispaniola* came from the cabin. I had to feel my way around on the deck. From the cabin came the sound of cursing and fighting. The two pirates were still at it. But what would happen when they stopped fighting?

I was afraid. I had a gun. But what good was one gun against two men? Any minute, I thought, they will come out on the deck. When they see what has happened to the ship . . . and if they find me . . .

My first thought was to find a place to hide. I could not stay on the deck. And I could not go near the cabin. Then I thought of just the right place— the apple barrel! It had worked for me before.

I made my way across the deck without a sound. Then I went down the steps to the kitchen. I stopped to listen a minute. Hearing nothing, I climbed into the apple barrel.

I was very tired by this time. It had been a very long day for me. Soon the rolling of the ship rocked me to sleep.

When I woke up, I did not know where I was at first. The apples in the barrel brought me back. I kept still and listened for the pirates. But since I heard nothing, I climbed out of the barrel.

I walked to the kitchen window and looked out. It was morning. And the *Hispaniola* was still moving. But the tide had not carried her out to sea. She had sailed to the other end of the island!

I still heard no sounds coming from the rest of the ship. It was much too quiet for my liking. Had the pirates killed each other? Or were they just sleeping off the rum? Afraid though I was, I would have to find out.

I went up the steps to the deck. But I stopped just inside the door to listen. I heard nothing. So I went out on the deck.

I saw the two pirates right away. They lay face down on the deck near the cabin. They were not moving. And the deck all around them was covered with blood. They must be dead, I thought. They must have killed one another.

As I walked over to them, I thought I saw one of them move. I stopped and watched. He was moving. He was trying to get up. And I knew his face. It was Israel Hands. Israel was the man who had told Silver he should kill me and my friends. I had heard him say that the first time I hid in the apple barrel.

But Israel Hands was not about to kill anyone now. He was not strong enough to get up. He was even too far gone to show surprise at seeing me there. All he could say was, "Rum! Rum! Rum!"

I went into the cabin and found a bottle with some rum left in it.

Back on deck, I went to the water barrel and took a drink. Then I went over to Israel and handed him the bottle. He drank the rum like a wild man.

"I needed that," he said, throwing the bottle away.

"Are you hurt much?" I asked him.

"Bad enough," he answered. Then he pointed to the man next to him. "But not as bad as him. He is dead for sure. And he should be for knifing old Israel Hands.

"And what might you be doing here, Jim Hawkins?" he asked.

I looked him straight in the eye. "I came on board to take over this ship," I answered. "From now on, Israel Hands, I am captain of the *Hispaniola*."

He gave me a very ugly look. But he did not say anything. My guess was that he still felt far from strong. I could see where a knife had cut into his leg. He must have lost a lot of blood.

"As captain," I went on, "I will not fly the pirate flag. The first thing I'll do is take down that flag."

I pulled down the pirate flag and threw it into the sea. "God save King George!" I cried.

Israel Hands sat up. "Well, Captain Hawkins," he said, "I see you have the best of me. And now I be thinking you will want to go back to the island. You will need my help to do that. I'll help you. But you will have to help me, too."

"What kind of help do you want me to give *you*?" I asked.

"I need food and water," he answered. "And I need something to cover the cut in my leg."

"All right," I said. "I am willing to help you. But you must do what I tell you to do. I want to sail this ship to North Inlet and beach it there. And I don't want any tricks from you!"

"Tricks!" cried Israel Hands. "What kind of tricks would I be playing on you? Why, I am so weak my own mother would not know me. I'll sail the *Hispaniola* any place you ask me to, Captain Hawkins."

"Very well," I said. "Let's get started. Then I will give you the things you need."

We sailed along the coast of Treasure Island with no trouble at all. I had brought food and water to Israel Hands. And I had helped him cover the deep cut in his leg. He looked almost well again. I sailed the ship. And he told me how to do it.

Late that afternoon, we came to North Inlet. "We made it! We made it!" I cried. Soon, I thought, I will be back with my friends. And I will bring them the happy news that we have the *Hispaniola*!

Israel Hands pulled himself up from the deck. "Well done, Captain Hawkins," he said. "This be North Inlet, all right. And I know a fine spot to beach the ship. Just you do as I tell you."

It is hard work beaching a ship as big as the *Hispaniola*. I did everything just as Israel told me to do. And at last she was headed straight for the beach on a big wave.

I was so busy at the ship's wheel that I did not think about Israel. But all at once, I had the strange feeling that someone was behind me. I turned around and there was Israel—with a long knife in his hand!

I pulled out my gun and pointed it at him. "Stop where you are!" I cried. "This gun is loaded and I will use it."

Israel kept coming for me. I fired the gun. But nothing happened. I fired again. But still it did not go off. The water, I thought, the water last night! The gun got wet in the water. It must be loaded again before it will fire.

Israel laughed. Knife in hand, he moved across the deck. I ran away from him. And he followed close behind me.

It was then that the *Hispaniola* hit the beach. She hit hard and turned on her side. Both Israel and I were knocked off our feet. Together we rolled across the deck to the side of the ship. Rolling with us was the dead pirate!

I was the first on my feet, for the dead man had landed on Israel. But with the *Hispaniola* on her side, I could not run on the deck. I went to the mast and began to climb it. I did not stop climbing until I came to the top.

I was over the water now. And it was a long drop down. I would have to make my stand on the mast. Israel was on his feet and headed for the mast. Soon he would be climbing up after me.

I pulled out the gun and went to work. As I loaded, I kept one eye on Israel. He was climbing the mast now, his knife between his teeth. My hands were shaking. But I got the gun loaded in time.

And it was just in time. Israel was not more than ten feet away. He had the knife in his right hand, ready to kill me.

"Come one more foot and I'll blow your head off!" I cried.

He stopped. And a weak smile came across his ugly face. "I guess you be winning after all, Jim," he said. Then he put his hands up, as if to show it was all over.

But it was just another trick. His knife sang through the air and hit me in the shoulder. At the same time, to my great surprise, my gun went off. With a loud cry, Israel fell head first into the water.

15 Pieces of Eight

Sitting on the *Hispaniola*'s mast, I watched Israel Hands hit the water far below me. He came up once for air. Then I saw him no more.

My shoulder felt as if it were on fire. Hot blood ran down my chest. And I almost blacked out when I pulled the knife out of my shoulder. But I was more afraid of falling from the mast than anything else. I knew I had to get down right away.

I was shaking all over. I had to rest a while before I tried to climb down the mast. In a few minutes, I felt a little better. Then I made my way back to the deck.

The first thing I did was take care of my shoulder. The cut hurt very much. But it was not very deep.

I went to the front of the ship and looked over the side. The water was not very deep there. I could see bottom. So, I threw over a line and climbed down. My shoulder hurt as I climbed down. But the water felt good and warm as I made my way to the beach.

It took me a long time to find my way to the fort. It was a good thing for me I had seen the treasure map. Without knowing the hills and the coast, I would have been lost for sure.

Something seemed strange to me when I came to the fort. No one was keeping watch.

I went over the fence without making a sound. Then I climbed the hill and listened outside the cabin door. Everything was quiet inside. Well, I thought, they could all be sleeping. But I still thought it was strange.

The door to the cabin was open. Quiet as a mouse, I stepped inside. But I had not gone far when my foot hit something soft.

All at once, a loud voice cried out. "Pieces of eight! Pieces of eight! Pieces of eight." It was Long John Silver's parrot, Captain Flint!

Then I heard the voice of Silver himself. "Who is there?" he cried.

I turned to run. But it was too late. Someone grabbed me from behind, and I could not move.

"Bring a light, Dick!" cried Silver. And soon another pirate stood in front of me with a light.

I felt sick as I looked around the room. The pirates held the cabin and all the stores. I saw no sign of my friends. Had they been killed by the pirates?

"Well, well, look who we have here," said Silver. "It is Jim Hawkins. Have you come for a visit, Jim?"

I said nothing. Silver sat down, with Captain Flint on his shoulder. The man looked old and tired to me now. He seemed to be thinking for a minute. Then he said, "I'll tell you how matters stand, my boy. Your friends were very angry when they found you had run away. They said they were through with you."

There was no answer I could give to this. I had thought my friends would be angry at my running off alone. But I was glad to learn that they were not dead.

Silver went on. "No, Jim, you can not go back to your friends now. They don't want you any more. It looks like you will have to come over to our side." Silver was smiling as he talked. But he could not hide his real feelings in his voice.

I was afraid. But I tried not to show it. "I will give you an answer," I said. "But first I have a right to know what has happened here. Why are you in the fort? And where are my friends?"

Silver thought for a minute. Then he smiled and began his story. "Early this morning, Doctor Livesey came down to the beach. He was carrying a white flag. 'Captain Silver,' he says to me, 'your men have sold you out. Look—the *Hispaniola* is gone!'

"Now me and my men had been drinking a bit of rum that night. And with singing and sleeping and all, we had not kept watch. We looked out, and sure enough the ship was gone.

"Then Doctor Livesey says, 'I think it is time we talked things over.' So we talked, the doctor and me. And you can see here what came of our talk. We got the fort and the stores. The doctor and the others saved their lives. We let them get away."

"Did Doctor Livesey say anything else?" I asked.

"I'll tell you what he said, word for word," answered Silver. "He said, 'As for that boy, I don't know where he is. And what is more, I don't care. We are sick of him!' Those were his very words."

"And now I guess I have to give you my answer," I said.

"That is right," said Silver. "You can come over to our side, or . . . "

"I have a few things I want to tell you, Silver," I said. "And it may put things in another light. The first is this. You are in a pretty bad way here. You have lost your ship. You have lost the treasure. And you have lost many men. Do you know who brought all this about? Well, it was me!

"I was hiding in the apple barrel the night we anchored off Treasure Island. I heard the plans you and your men were making. And I told my friends all about it. As for the *Hispaniola*, I cut her anchor rope. And I killed the two men you left on board her.

"I am not afraid of you. I have had the laugh on you all the time. You can kill me now if you like. But it will not do you any good. Let me go, and I will put in a good word to save *your* lives."

Silver had a strange look on his face. I could not tell how he took what I said. But by now, the other pirates were angry.

"There is more to his story," said one of them. "It was him that knew Billy Bones and Pew!"

"And it was him that took the map from Billy's sea chest!" said another. "First and last, Jim Hawkins has done us in."

"Now it is him who will be done in!" cried the first pirate. And he pulled out a knife. He was ready to spring at me. But Long John Silver stopped him.

"Hold on there!" roared Silver. "Who do you think you are, Tom Morgan? You think you are the captain now? Let me put you straight on that. Silver is captain here. Cross me, would you? Many a good man has tried that before. And where are they now? Feeding the fishes, that is where."

The pirates did not like this at all. "Tom is right," said one of them. "Run the boy through!"

Silver gave them all a hard look. "Do any of you want to have it out with me then?" he cried. "Take up a sword if you do. I'll see the color of your insides!"

Not one of the men moved.

"So that is the way it is," said Silver. "You are all good with your mouths. But you are not much with a sword. Now hear this. I am still captain here. The man who lays a hand on Jim Hawkins answers to me."

Silver took me to the side of the room. "Now listen to me, Jim Hawkins," he said in my ear. "Those men want your hide. But Long John Silver has always been your friend. I like you, Jim. If you stand by me, I'll stand by you."

"I'll do what I can," I told him.

"Good!" said Silver. "I am on your side now. You have the *Hispaniola*. And I don't know where it is. But I know when the game is up. That I do."

Silver looked across the room at the men. Then he turned back to me. "Why did Doctor Livesey give me the map, Jim?" he asked.

The surprise on my face was enough to answer him.

Before long, Silver and the other men went back to sleep. But I could not fall asleep right away. I kept thinking of the surprising game Silver was playing. He was trying to be on both sides at the same time!

16 Treasure Hunt

Nothing happened that night in the fort. We were all sound asleep until morning. When we woke up, it was to a voice calling from the jungle. "Hello! Hello! You inside the fort! It is Doctor Livesey."

And Doctor Livesey it was. He came over the fence and up the hill to the cabin.

"Top of the morning to you, Doctor!" cried out Silver. "How are you this fine morning? We have a surprise for you, sir. We have a new man in our crew here. I believe he is an old friend of yours."

"Not Jim?" asked the doctor.

"The very same," said Silver. "And a good night's sleep he has had with us. Come in. I'll let you talk to the boy. But first you must take care of my men."

I was very happy to see the good doctor. It was all I could do to keep from crying. After he had doctored the pirates, we went outside to talk.

"Well, Jim," said Doctor Livesey, "I am glad to see you are all right. But look at the trouble you got into by running away!"

Before I knew it, I was crying like a baby. "Oh, doctor," I said, "I know I should not have gone off alone. But I am not afraid for my own skin. I would be dead already were it not for Silver. I am only afraid they will do something to make me talk. They will find out where I hid the *Hispaniola!* I left her beached in North Inlet."

"Then it was you who took the ship!" said the doctor.

I told Doctor Livesey all about Ben Gunn's boat. I told him how I had gone to the *Hispaniola* and cut her anchor rope. I told him about the pirates on board and how I killed Israel Hands. I also told him about the strange things Silver had been saying to me.

Doctor Livesey was very moved by my story. "Jim," he said, "you have saved our lives at every step of the way. We can never thank you enough. We have made plans. But I can not tell you what they are. Just keep your head, Jim. And don't run away again!"

Then Doctor Livesey called for Silver. "Silver," he said to him, "I have something to tell you. And it is this. Don't be in a great hurry to find the treasure."

"Doctor," said Silver, "you don't know what you are saying. Why, finding the treasure is the only way to save Jim and me. If we don't find it right away, those men will kill us both!"

"Very well," said the doctor, "go if you must. But be careful when you find it. You might find trouble, too. I can not say any more. But keep Jim close to you. If we get out of this with our lives, I'll try to save you. You have my word on that."

Silver smiled the way he used to in the old days on board the *Hispaniola*. "Thank you, sir!" he said. "Thank you very much. Your word is as good as gold to me."

With that, we walked Doctor Livesey down to the fence. He was soon over the fence and into the jungle.

Back inside the cabin, Silver kept up a running line of talk. He was full of plans for each of us. The men felt better now. They were even laughing and joking. Soon all were ready to begin hunting for the buried treasure.

They were a strange-looking crew. What clothes they had were full of holes. And many had lost their shoes and hats. They shouldered picks. But they were also armed to the teeth with swords and guns!

For strange looks, though, no one could top Long John Silver. He had a gun hanging across his chest. And he had a gun hanging down his back. He also had guns in the right and left pockets of his coat. A sword was hanging from his side. Sitting on his shoulder was his parrot, Captain Flint.

Silver carried one end of a rope. And I was tied to its other end—like a dancing bear. Hopping along on his crutch, he was something to see!

All morning we marched through the jungle. The pirates stopped often. They would look at the map. And they would talk and point. Then they would look at the map again. From what I could hear, we were heading for Spyglass Hill.

A red X on the map showed where the biggest part of the treasure was. It was between the beach and Spyglass Hill. But it was a big X on a small map. There was writing on the back of the map, too. But it was not at all clear in what it said. It said something about a "tall tree" on "Spyglass shoulder." I guessed they were looking for a tall tree on the shoulder of Spyglass Hill.

It was not until the afternoon that we left the jungle behind us. But we still had a good climb to the shoulder of Spyglass Hill. Many a man wished he had not had rum the night before.

Up we went for another hour to the shoulder of the hill. But when we got there, no one could tell which tree was the "tall tree." Silver thought about this for a while. Then he sent the men into all parts of the woods to look. Before long, one of them let out a great cry.

"What is it?" called Silver, running to the man. "Have you found something?"

The man had found something. But he was so afraid, he could not talk. What he found was a tall tree, all right. But at the foot of the tree lay a man's skeleton!

Silver took a careful look at the skeleton. It looked as if it had been there a long time. "This would be one of the men who landed with Flint," he said.

Silver took the treasure map from his pocket and opened it. He looked at the map. Then he looked at the skeleton. "Flint used a dead man to point the way to his treasure," he said. "See the red X on the map? Now look which way the skeleton's feet are pointing. That would be Flint's little joke."

We took up the march again. But the men were not the happy crew that started out. They were afraid now. The skeleton had started them all thinking. It was Captain Flint they were afraid of. And that was all they could talk about.

"Flint is dead," said Silver. "I saw him with my own eyes. Let's go after the treasure!"

"If ever a dead man came back, it would be Flint," said one man.

"Yes," said another. "And if he killed six men here once, he could do it again."

The pirates did not care about the treasure any more. They thought only of their own skins. But they were afraid to go back to the fort alone. They walked on, looking to each side and behind them.

We had not gone very far when we stopped to rest. It was then that a thin, high voice called out from the woods. "Darby McGraw! Darby McGraw! Bring me the rum, Darby!"

"Flint!" cried one of the men. "Them was Flint's last words!"

The pirates began to run away. Their eyes were almost popping from their heads.

"Wait!" cried Silver. "That don't sound like Flint's voice to me."

"Come on, Silver!" said one of the men.

"Let's get out of this cursed place!" said another.

"Leave the treasure where it is!" another cried.

"No!" roared Silver. "Be quiet, you yellow dogs! That is not Flint's voice at all. But we have all heard it before, that be sure. . . . It sounds like . . . Why, it sounds like Ben Gunn!"

"Yes!" cried one of the pirates. "Ben Gunn! It was Ben Gunn's voice."

"But Gunn could not be here any more than Flint could," said another man.

"Right you are," said Silver. "And no one is afraid of Ben Gunn, living or dead."

This seemed to make the pirates feel better again. But they had to have a meeting to talk things over. It took some time before we went on.

And the place where the treasure was buried was not far away. Before long, we spotted a small clearing in the woods. "That is it!" said Silver. "The map shows the treasure to be right up there."

With loud and happy cries, the pirates ran to the clearing. Silver and I hurried on behind them. We saw them come to the clearing and stop. And then they became very quiet. It was strange.

It took a minute or two to catch up with the others. And when we did, we could not believe our eyes. No wonder the pirates were standing around not saying a word. Where the treasure should have been, there was nothing but a hole in the ground!

We could all see what had happened. This was no new hole. There was grass growing in it. And beside it were part of an old pick and old boards. The boards had once been part of boxes. On one of them was the word *Walrus*, the name of Flint's ship. Captain Flint's treasure had been found years before we came to Treasure Island. It was all gone!

17 The End of My Story

The pirates stood looking at the hole as if someone had hit them. Then one of them jumped into it. Cursing, he started to dig with his hands. After a minute, he stood up again. He had a gold piece in his hand. "So this is your treasure, Silver?" he asked. "Is this what has come of all your big talk? Do you see what your pretty plans have brought us?"

"It is those two who got us into all this!" cried another man. He cursed Silver and me. Then he pulled out his sword.

"What are we waiting for?" cried another pirate. "Let's run them through!"

All at once, the five pirates ran at us. But before they could attack, there was a roar of guns. Two of the pirates fell. The others ran into the woods. Then, from the woods behind us, came Doctor Livesey, Jack, and Ben Gunn.

"You were just in time!" cried Silver. "That were a close call, it were. And there you are, Ben Gunn! I would guess it was you who took the treasure."

"I be the one, Mr. Silver," said Ben, turning red in the face.

"He has been alone on this island for three years," said Doctor Livesey. "He found the treasure. That is, he found the biggest part of it. All he had to do was dig it up and hide it in another spot."

On the way to the beach, Doctor Livesey told us the rest of the story. The night I ran away, Ben told him about taking the treasure. It was in his cave. That was why they had let Silver take over the fort. They all went to Ben's cave. There was food there. And they could all keep watch on the treasure.

The map was of no use any more. So the doctor gave that to Silver, too. But then he found me at the fort with the pirates. He had to plan a way to save me.

Ben tried to make the pirates afraid of Captain Flint first. That was to give Doctor Livesey time to bring Jack back to help. He came back just when the pirates were attacking me and Silver.

"It is a good thing I had Jim with me," said Silver. "You would have let Long John be cut to pieces. And you would never give it another thought."

"Not a thought at all," answered Doctor Livesey, laughing.

Ben Gunn's cave was near the beach. When we got there, Squire Trelawney was keeping watch outside. He was angry when he saw Silver. "They say I am not to turn you in when we get home," he said. "Very well. I shall do as they ask. But may God's curse be on you!"

"Yes, sir. Thank you, sir," said Silver.

This made the squire very angry. He would have hit Silver had the doctor not stepped between them.

We went into Ben's cave. There, in front of a big fire, lay Captain Smollett. He was better now. But he still had to rest most of the time. Across from him, shining in the light from the fire, was the treasure.

I never knew there could be so many gold pieces! And there were gold bars laid one on top of another. Rings, cups, bowls, cut stones, and other beautiful things lay to one side. I could not believe my eyes.

That night, my friends brought the *Hispaniola* from North Inlet. And the next morning, we began loading her with the treasure. Silver helped with the work. But, for the most part, he tried to stay out of our way. No one had a kind word for him.

It took a few days to move all the treasure to the ship. The gold bars were very heavy. In that time, not a word was heard from the other pirates. It was not until we set sail from the island that we saw them again. They were on the beach as we sailed by, waving to us. They called for us to come back for them.

But we could not take them with us. They might try to take over the ship again. Doctor Livesey called out to them. He told them to go to Ben's cave. He told them they would find food and guns there.

When they saw that we would not come back for them, they began cursing us. One of them had a gun. He fired at us and hit our sail. But they could not hurt us. That was the last we would ever see of them.

There were only five of us to sail the ship. (Captain Smollett still could not move about.) For the long trip to England, we needed help. So, we headed for a place where we could take on more men.

In a few days, we came to a town on the coast of Mexico. We were all very tired. But we were glad to see people again. We landed right away. I went with the doctor and the squire. And we stayed on land all night.

We were not too surprised at what happened while we were gone. "Silver is gone," Ben Gunn told us. "He got away on me. But me thinks we are well off without him. Oh, yes. And he took a bag of gold pieces with him."

Ben Gunn was right, we all felt. We would be better off without Long John Silver. And one bag of gold pieces was not too much to pay for that.

We took on our new hands. And then we sailed for England. It was a good trip. Before long, we were in Bristol once again.

Each of us got a part of the treasure. We used it, for good or bad, as we saw fit. We never heard of Silver again. He and his parrot may still be living in some part of the world. Who knows? He may even be sailing the seas looking for more buried treasure.

I have told you of my first and last trip to hunt for treasure. Though there is still more gold on the island, I will never make another trip. I have had enough of that. But sometimes at night I hear the sound of the waves on Treasure Island. It turns my blood cold. Sometimes the voice of Captain Flint rings in my ears. "Pieces of eight!" cries the parrot. "Pieces of eight! Pieces of eight! Pieces of eight!"